HOW TO MAKE CURRY GOAT

Louise McStravick

First published 2020 by Fly on the Wall Press

Published in the UK by

Fly on the Wall Press

56 High Lea Rd

New Mills

Derbyshire

SK22 3DP

www.flyonthewallpoetry.co.uk

ISBN: 978-1-913211-19-6

Typesetting and Cover Design by Isabelle Kenyon.

Supported using public funding by
ARTS COUNCIL ENGLAND

LOTTERY FUNDED

Acknowledgements

To my family who have always been there. My Erdington Kwick Save car park girls- we still here even if the Kwick Save is not.

To those who I've voice-noted poems and whose feedback has helped me to think about things in ways I wouldn't have otherwise, you know who you are.

Thanks to the editors of the following publications where some of these poems have appeared, Dear Damsels, Porridge Magazine, Lacuna Lit, Words on Windrush Anthology.

Praise for 'How To Make Curry Goat'

"In these delicately observed poems, Louise McStravick explores the landscape of her heritage and identity; painting an incisive and affectionate portrait of the people she has encountered along the way. These poems are vivid, sensual and rich in imagery and they pull no punches. Whilst each poem is a delicious treat in its own right, collectively they constitute a brave and important story, beautifully and boldly told. This is a recipe book for the soul and the senses and the poems will linger with you long after the book has been returned to the shelf."

- Mary Dickins, Author of Happiness FM, Burning Eye Books

"Louise McStravick invites us into her world as a daughter of the Windrush generation, with a sharp observation and a dry sense of humour. We meet family, friends and errant lovers in poems of wit and sensuality, and in McStravick's vivid imagery and often surprising language we learn to smell, taste and enjoy this Goat Stew as she explores the feelings of belonging and alienation that beset her. A wonderful first collection."

- Janice Dempsey, Co-Publisher at Dempsey & Windle

"How to Make Curry Goat is a lively and warm-hearted exploration of identity, appetite, love and loss. These poems are frank, funny and richly sensory; Louise McStravick is an acute observer of the world around her."

- Dr Megan Hayes, Lecturer in Creative Writing, Teeside University

Contents

Just another road in Erdington

Tiny meows from tattered sofa,

patterned black as the 80s,

they like dark spaces, privacy for the mother, sacred,

good job our sofa had holes in it created

by children who did not see the value in 80s chic.

The first thing those kittens see is darkness,

I am not sure they care for 80s upholstery either.

Years later, black relic of the 80s, a torch in our back garden

blackened bones,

carcass left in grass Savannah-long,

we exotic like Africa;

Friends think it's a country. So did we for a while.

My dad's from Jamaica.

We back and forth, wear countries like

badges of honour.

One time M got beaten up until

his body almost gave up.

Tubes replace spoons for he whose

body learned burglary, its pursuit.

His mom carried a dirty gift to her son in prison.
A mother's love does not have to agree with the law.
Now visiting times are split in two places
that family ought to stop getting caught.

One time boys set fire to the fields out back
but I'm not supposed to know that.
Bushcraft for kids, urban survival is a lot like this.

We would play tracking, ackee one two three,
dug ditches that swallowed dogs whole for a week
then spat them back into our welcoming arms.

My sister said J's house smells like crack.
She's 10 years older and older means wiser and wiser means right
and I am not one to compete with that.
Our nostrils have not yet learned to be wise.

A sister got kicked out by her mother
and got pregnant with her lover
who showed her how heroin can make the world stop shouting.
The kids were taken away. *He in prison.*

She always scared me at school,

she cool drinking vodka from plastic water bottle and no maths.

Something to aspire to.

Now her shadow asks for money with a mouth that moves but does not speak.

J's house got rushed once and they locked his mom in the cupboard.

I heard. Nothing is sacred.

Our house got rushed too. I no longer answer front doors.

One time when we were 9, C next door dropped

my brother from his shoulders and his face fell away.

We would hear their dog's screams in our sleep after

their dad beat its barks away.

One day it went silent.

He used to knock unannounced and announce to my mom his affections,

said his wife wasn't giving enough attention.

When he died, his hedge grew so long it blocked out the sunlight.

When I stay over, I am strangled by darkness.

I wonder if this is what being alive feels like.

Sometimes the only thing I hear at night is my blood.

B up the road is still alive, in his 80's still smokes,

has stopped perving mainly because he sleeps all the time.

When we were younger he was so complimentary,

I prefer him now, sedentary.

He sells my mom cheap cigarettes.

I hear her cough in my sleep.

Two witches used to live on the street,

their hair had white streaks

and they would scare children with their silence;

they had no sweets.

One day they were in the newspaper,

gassed in their garage, suicide, death, violent.

We regret calling them witches.

One time, I went missing. I was not aware,

I was up K's house looking at records.

My sister found me there.

One time, my mom went missing. I had to climb through the kitchen.

Plant pot crime scene victim

decapitated on floor, brown blood, evidence all over the front room.

Dad found her in the police station.

It was a fight over the garden fence.

Mom's got a transfer,
housing association Sutton Coldfield,
nice road cinema and shop front lights on with hairdressers and nice pubs.
Everything different.

We cannot bring ourselves to leave.

Tanned feet

This tan from Jamaica never washed off
it sticks on skin still salty from floating in warm waters
that hugged each part of this body
that found its way there.

The smell of citrus fruit, fried plantain and smoked wood
still fresh in nostrils that have been cleared of soot and grey air
for the first time

with every breath I smell lime.
This tongue tastes the tang tantalising, it salivates
as it rises to the call
'hot sauce, sweet sauce'
and asks for both.

I hope that life is not too hard here.

Words formed through lips that have welcomed
guava picked with my father's hand
straight from the tree they were birthed
and they speak of a different me

this tan has not faded from feet

that discovered ground

that saw a 12-year-old boy run from a

grandfather who only spoke the language of pain,

whose grandmother's strength was grown from salt earth,

enough to water a boy for more years than

a mother and a father combined,

who waved that boy away with a salt-coloured flag.

These tanned feet have grown golden next to

the ghost of a mango tree

where children would meet,

bodies speak the language of freedom

run to catch shrimp in a river that

only runs now in black and white memories.

But my feet see them in colour

in the soft, brown warmth of a tan

nourished with coconut jelly

so it does not fade

that will be topped up again

one day.

I am teaching at a summer school in Italy (again)

The corridors need a lick of paint,
the walls are crumbling;
I am late, but that is nothing new.
Tinged yellow, what was once
fresh now has a hint of mildew,
but that's OK, the building still stands.
The grounds are fat with grass that should
have been cut weeks ago,
it scratches these legs that kick the ball,
muscle memory of secondary, year 8
right wing midfield,
it never goes where it is supposed to.
But that's OK, they still stand.
Wire-strong black hairs wear this home,
they would once have been driven out,
scraped with a blunt blade on
raw skin, black raining down on
white porcelain, no time to rinse.

I slap the bite of the mosquito
they are still hot for the taste of this
blood,
warm, sticky,

some things never change.

Some things do and I

am not sure which way is best,

whether blackboards are better

for the environment,

chalk never seems to last,

but it comes from the earth,

porous, it drinks water

like a 32-year-old hangover.

Names fossilised into tables,

Paulo, Gianluca, Beatrice. Catzo!

80s wooden chairs too stiff to be practical.

Do these walls look better

with their skin peeling?

Blinds hanging down like

an insult on this body,

they do not stop the light

from getting into my eyes.

Perhaps a bit of paint

is all it needs.

Earl Grey Tea

Mid 2000s, Em and Ash are washing dishes
with washing powder, we proper adults like 17
and the smell of green sinks into fibres and voices.
We listen to Dizzee Sidewinder and drink vodka and coke
and make loud noises like gun-fingers that cut through haze smoke.

She asks if I want tea,
she says they only have Earl Grey, something strange
not like builder's brown brewed,
My mom always said I can't make tea, I like it stewed.
Do I like milk with it? she asks.
I do not know, is this regal tea like builder's brown?
If so, then just a dash.

It tastes like a field of tea-shaped flowers
sharp on my tongue like my inability
to use the word *'lend'* correctly.
I have a degree in English, don't you know.
My voice sounds like I'm stoned, they told me,
can't you be less Brummie, it's a bit deep, doesn't go.

2018, proper adult cohabiting, he would choose
Earl Grey before breakfast, naturally,

one tea bag breakfast

one tea bag regal in his family.

He didn't drink builder's brown brewed, he liked his

Earl Grey in a teapot stewed.

I fill my mouth with flowery tea: hold it,

let it ruminate, evaporate, sink deep into taste buds

so I can speak more pretty.

He taught me how to use the word *lend* correctly.

Now every time my tongue speaks

flowery, this is his legacy.

I no more builder's brown brewed

I breathe regal breath with bergamot-scented hues.

Spices

Fenugreek leaves,
coriander seeds
cumin in a jar
fennel
cayenne pepper
curry powder, brand Rajah.
My arsenal
no recipe can defeat
I shoot them down,
with dried curry leaves.

My heavy hands
douse energetically,
nostrils warm
I've created
something fragrant for tea.

I push packets into
the box with the red lid
then close it
heavy hands spilt
chilli over the spices
oops, secret doses.

Now the red-lidded box

sits quiet, unopened

it whispers of hands

that once created

dishes that danced

on tongues

that moved for each other

that said,

That was delicious,

Thanks,

I'll wash up,

No, it's OK, you sit down.

There is no place

for these chilli-laced spices

they have nowhere left to go.

They no longer

dance on tongues,

they no longer

speak of home.

How to make curry goat

Take around 7 quid's worth of goat

Or mutton dem di same ting

A spring of thyme, two large onions, three if you're that way inclined

Not di Spanish h'onion di British h'onion.

A bulb of garlic. All-purpose seasoning and Caribbean Curry Powder

It nah matter which curry powder you fi use.

Using eyes to measure, one-part All Purpose to two-part curry powder

Be careful with the All Purpose. You nah want too much salt.

Sprinkle it over the meat in a zig-zag motion get your hands in until you

have an even coating. Be sure to have washed the meat first.

British people nah wash dem meat, it nasty, that's how dem get mad cow disease.

Slice the onions into strips

You nah want them too small, or dem fi disappear.

Dice the garlic.

You affi crush it first, cho!

Chop the Scotch bonnet

Dependin' on how much pepper you want, me nah like too much pepper

Do not ask questions on precise measurements

You ask too many question!

Or whether or not to use oil

You chat too much!

Or why he says goat is the same as mutton.

Dem di same ting!

Even though one's a goat and one's a sheep.

Dem taste di same!

Proceed to throw the meat into the pan (no oil)

You affi turn it!

Don't expect him to explain this is a descriptive process.

Nah ask me nah question.

Turn the heat down low and add the onion, garlic, chilli and thyme into the pan.

You can add a likkle bita fresh ginger as well.

Grate in fresh ginger and put the lid on. Do not ask why he bangs the lid with a wooden spoon.

Nah ask me nah question.

Now wait.

And wait.

And wait.

Do not ask if it's ready yet.

Nah ask me no question.

Do not try to sneak a piece of meat when he isn't looking. He is always looking.

It nah ready yet!

Go upstairs to ignore the feeling of stomach eating itself through the

nostrils revealing the taste to tongue that hungers only for this.

And wait.

Tell your tongue to stop dribbling spit

that good things come to those that wait, imagine the plate, the tempting

fate that would be you trying to steal meat again.

It nah ready yet!

And wait.

You are 6 again, 8 again, 10, again, 14, again,

waiting, waiting, salivating sitting on hands that do not know how to

wait.

He calls you to taste, it tastes better than great

it tastes like from the plate of his mom I never knew,

his gran, my namesake, it tastes like it has travelled on vibrations, on

waves, a land foreign to new territory.

Indentured slavery mixed with imported trade makes its way to my plate:

new learned memories.

Now these hands follow those that for centuries have taught their

daughters, their sons, me to make this curry.

Goat,

I watch as he sucks marrow from bone and takes my bones off me.

Gross,

one day I will tell my daughter, my son to stop asking questions,

I will move slow with hands that think with this memory.

Intuition in the acquisition of learned rhythms.

I will tell them to wait. And wait and wait.

Until. Our story rises with steam from the plate.

Mommy belly

Your mommy belly
looks back at me with
a hundred smiles,
carved by my brother, sister and I.
As soft as the pastry we press together, hands blessed with
blood that runs thicker.
We play with the pastry after
making figures out of the alchemy
of flour and egg and water.

When we press, we're impressed
at how our fingers stay,
even when pulled away and
we learn the beauty of soft things.

We learn the beauty of belly with skin
that no longer fits.
That does not conform to the rules of playdough
it does not return to its original shape, no
more like a creased cape now
on the world's greatest superhero.

I marvel as it tells the story of me breech,

brought out in a glory of blood and guts

your belly cut to reveal my first cries

we fly together you and I,

you tell me how we almost died

many times.

You returned to hospital after 5 days

scar that once smiled, now weeping,

me sleeping beauty at home

blissful ignorance at the war you fought

to get me out, breathing air.

Your body would return battle-scarred,

forever marked your reward,

Stolen sleep night feeds messy rooms demanding food play-fights screams
and bites, power rangers don't talk to strangers broken bed sore head
sex talk pep talks boyfriends bad friends keeping you up all night all over
again.

This skin, some would say ruined,

it does not fit, it hangs with lines still red

as you are tiny and I had a big head

big body, a large 8 pounds, they said.

You made the impossible possible,

and so is written the improbable

burnt into skin.

Of what was once in, now out
pressing, wondering how I fit in,
wondering if my skin will do the same.

When I see the first sign on thigh,
a line red and angry
at my body for no longer being defined as a child,
there is no denial
I will grow a mommy belly too
it's genetic.

My belly will hang like the creased cape of a superhero
that has held the world within,
it will not return to its original shape, no
this living, breathing
skin.

When I see celebrities on the telly,
one day after with laughter,
flat belly smooth skin and I think
we aren't beautiful.
I forget the beauty of soft things
I want hard abs and elastic band skin
that snaps back quicker than a
Snapchat…

Your mommy belly tells me I can't have that.

But what is more beautiful than a body

whose lines spell out the story of our lives.

That shows us the changes,

the lines on our faces, the softness of skin,

the stretch marks burnt in,

this living, breathing thing.

Evolving because we are

superheroes.

So, I want your mommy belly and when I do

I will press it with my fingers

and it will remind me of you.

Fatherland, Motherland

Fields of sugarcane, fertilised by the graves of slaves
who worked all their days,
down the road from where my father's from,
Crofts Hill, Clarendon.
Abundantly, banana trees, coconut palms and guava leaves,
hang a world away from Rubicon.
Scoop out the coconut jelly with
makeshift machete-made spoons once done,
ready to line the stage for the graves of my ancestors.
1898 the birth of my namesake
50 years from the emancipation of slaves.
this woman who raised my father,
a generation away from a pain
not in our memories, but I believe
I must remember this part of my personal history
as I do, on the day of my grandmother's wake.

Prayer book air just circulates
and '*let mi tell you mi bredrins*' make up tributes to the saviour,
hallelujah and '*Yes Jesus, amuse me*',
a distant relative and stranger
to a culture I've longed for since I can remember.
Cousins and uncles I didn't realise were relatives

through the eyes of a young kid fast-talking

whatum bredrins curry goat and plantain.

Snapper with eyes watching

the smell of saltfish boiling

put me off seafood

'cus I could see the food looking

accusatory before we'd cook it.

Mutton patties and fry fish

my British friends

didn't understand him

the way we did

with his creole English.

patois, wha gwaans, dunzeye and chos,

integrate into the vernacular and soon afterwards

redefine what it means to be   English.

So here I am

in the fatherland, 7 miles of white sand,

familiar lilts in voices rising and falling

intertwined with the music of the waves and sellers calling.

Wondering if this is where I belong,

roadside shacks and dancehall songs,

or am I wrong to feel a part of it

an imposter with my

British   English.

So long wha gwaan blud in a Birmingham accent,
I'd never given much thought to what cultural appropriation meant,
is it a compliment dressed in a British accent
or detachment from the place it came from?

Immigration into assimilation
to become part of a 'Great Nation'
to become part of a population
hostile to the colours of Other,
'rivers of blood' among
green, yellow and black
different shades of Empire,
which required 'people for hire'
in exchange for indefinite
leave to remain.

No Irish, No blacks, No dogs.
Yet, Rule Britannia called out to us
with the promise of a mother's love.

But the mother didn't nurture us
from a motherland murderous

to the motherland's superfluous

we are the Lonely Londoners

playing dominoes with Island overtones

as the motherland nurtures us with

prospects, equal opportunities

government-sponsored university education and

lifetime Student loan fees

jerk chicken and carnival vibes

gang culture or knife crime

stop and searches and the white flight.

Jungalist massive; Garage raving

reggae and dancehall in Dalston dancing,

Grime MCs and Music made in basements,

the real punk movement pirate radio stations.

What have we left behind?

I thought I was culturally Jamaican

but I realised since I arrived, being second generation

has different connotations.

I am British, English, a bit Irish and Jamaican

wha gwaan blud

curry goat and plaintain,

garage, yorkshire puddings and grime

this is all part of my culture,

but which culture is mine?

Postcards from England

These postcard chimneys stand proud as steel,
Empire's arms open like a long-lost relative.
The smoke becomes a cloud to ride on,
high in the skies of prosperity,
a snapshot of opportunity.

We sunbathe in ship's shadows, absorb its promise
of hope, for young minds shown for the first time,
the world does not end,
at the line where the sea meets the sky.

When it is our time, on our ship,
our ears adjust to the sound
of voices that sing the song of the freedom beyond
the horizon. Our prayer offered to the skies.

I thought I was alone in this journey but the voices
speak familiarity, like old school friends.
You cannot quite put a name to the face,
but it reminds you of that time and that place.

The postcards did not show that breath
could appear like a duppy. Condensation
caught by cupped hands in front of face,
you get any warmth you can take in this place.

If they had told me, I would have brought a coat.

Train from Southampton to Paddington
on the left, I see chimneys a-plenty.
standing tall on buildings, proud as steel,
more factories than they have people in the
West Indies it seems.

My sister laughs at me and with her words that
rip through picture postcard memories,
These factories are homes!
Here they all have chimneys, burn coal,
breathe warmth in thick air.

I whisper words that land soft into ears of those
who fear our presence is too loud
who see the world in black and white
where I come from, we had so many colours
they spoiled my eyes.

There is no longer a line where the sea ends

and the sky begins - this line has been replaced by chimneys,

smoke steals oxygen from mouths that once spoke of ships.

This air feels too heavy for these bones,

I send postcards of chimneys to the people back home.

Love potion to get him back

Scrape the traces of your love-making,
don't pretend you've changed your sheets.
It's easy, just use the scalpel
you used to cut out your pulse
as an offering.

Find the hair you found
in the bathroom that wasn't yours.
Straight and conforming,
like your hairs never could be.
It was probably just your flatmate,
but you saw strange flesh flattened for him
sizzling. Served pink, just how he likes it.

Then take the ash he left in
your absence, incense inhaled
to get rid of your smell,
kindling tiny unmarked grave with
a gathering of mates who say
'well, if it wasn't right then
you did the right thing.'
They didn't realise he
inhaled freedom like it

doesn't kill in the end.

Add the leftover pasta and pesto
he made that you couldn't bring yourself
to throw away.
Choke on the green like
new beginnings and
regurgitate.

Put them in the bath, cold
a trickle of mockery,
soak with pieces of the fine
crockery from his parents
you'd never seen such fine crockery.
silly, really.

Imbibe the potion
ignore sickness rising to the surface
each item an island of regret.

Now rub until your
skin wears promise like
destiny.

Do not leave

Do not

leave.

Pasta, pesto, rocket and tomato

Only the best cherry tomatoes would do, Sainsbury's finest. That's the important part. I thought all tomatoes taste the same, but what would I know? I hadn't even eaten a cherry tomato until my sister went to uni and came back with exotic recipes.

Balsamic vinegar too. Another thing that's new. I love how you knew so many things, like who the owner of the Daily Mirror was.

High fibre spaghetti severed with scissors: you did not like to eat them whole. Too much like hard work. I should have known.

Red pesto not green.

Rocket leaves.

Freshly grated parmesan. A very expensive cheese.

Weekday meals sorted like easy, like waking up every day next to your sleeping face and poking 'til you wake.

Pasta pesto and tomatoes, like the way you move your toes so I can't help but kiss them

Worshipper of toes and ground and dishes with foreign ingredients.

I didn't eat pasta 'till Uni.

Halloumi neither nor coriander. Balsamic was an island somewhere.

You expensive taste, you with irresistible toes and poker face.

I throw the pasta pesto away, you expensive taste, you who walked away, who did not like to commit to your leftovers. Who would rather go back home with all your washing so that I can no longer smell your toes.

We were only two episodes away from the finale of series 5 of Buffy.

I wanted to surprise you with her sacrifice, the Gift. I wanted to share this. Spoiler alert, we didn't make it to the end.

Well you couldn't wait.

And I am more than a meal you make when you don't know what else to do.

Just buy Ottlenghi, you'll see what I should mean to you.

My favourite colour

I like silver glitter

That imagines cheekbones on

Faces of those made for filters.

I like pink but only

When you don't ask me.

And my favourite shade of lipstick is

Blood red,

The colour of all the men

I've conjured with my lips.

Peachy pink is best, the colour of

That doll's plastic skin,

Whose hair I cut until it pointed

Like a jagged joke,

From her crown.

I wondered why they made dolls

In pink and not brown.

I like blue more now

I never used to, because

Blue is the colour of sky,

And sky can suck you up

And spit you onto grey

Concrete

Smashed-up green like avocado on toast.

I think I belong in the sky now.

They don't agree

I give a solid concrete smile and they

Eat and they eat and they eat.

I always liked the way

Yellow is the colour of the sun

Which burns everything that enters it

You can't even get within

50 feet.

I think yellow is my favourite colour.

On the London Northwestern

Bedtime is for those who call people home,   (failed)

my sheets are angry they swallow me whole.   (empty)

The London Northwestern from Euston to Newstreet   (period pains)

an old friend I have become reaquainted with.   (sex)

We share body heat, I stand in the aisle   (men)

smiles remind my face can do the same,   (sex)

shelter, because of course there's rain,   (wet)

the warmth of breath and mind busied with conversations   (fit)

How many reps can you do?   (fit)

My arms are too wide for these seats.   (fit)

You're more hench than me.   (fit twat)

More interesting than a brain that only knows how to play   (fuck)

On a loop.   (fuck)

On a loop.   (fuck)

On a loop.   (shit)

There is no stop button.   (why)

I prefer the stiff truth of the seats, bottle green against my back, (fertility)

my bare arms welcome the rough and the   (Boyfriend)

window cold on a face that finds peace in   (I miss him)

hardness. That view though.   (sexual experimentation)

Who needs to be deceived by a pillow   (sex)

with its offer of kindness. Breakfast in bed.   (32)

I prefer the soft spoken lady, voice of comfort with   (marriage)

You are now arriving at Watford Junction.   (fuck)

Is that it?   (yes)

Loads of time left. I could do with a plug socket   (download Tinder)

but can't complain when this train was less than   (delete Tinder)

half the price of Virgin.   (sex)

Sometimes all I need is to be alone with all these people.   (sex)

I hear them in my sleep sometimes and I am reminded   (masturbate)

of my choice.   (32)

I could have settled for   (cohabiting)

the Victoria line followed by the 149.   (marriage)

instead I chose to end my nights,   (single)

on the London to Birmingham line.   (fuck)

My body is yours, please take it

My body is composed of words

'You are beautiful'

My limbs are pulled on strings

'You have such lovely hair'

I am wrapped up in silk spun from well-meaning mouths

'Bum ting'

Strong hands crafted my soft bones out of hard rib

'and they knew that they were naked'

My eyes create shapes I want to see

'you shouldn't have cut your hair'

Empty spaces are filled with the heaviness of expectation

'you have a moustache'

I stick a needle through my lips

'slut'

I camouflage myself in grey asphalt

'smile it isn't that bad'

and flowers

'suck my dick'

My body is written between the lines of verses and chapters

'life begins at conception'

signed under smiles and camera flashes

'Heartbeat Bill'

A luxury to be taxed.

'she gave me all of the tree and I did eat'

My steps are hallowed

'you think you're too nice'

My insides become uncertainty

'side effects include
depression,
breast cancer,
cervical cancer,
weight gain,
acne...'

I am made of thunderstorms

'is it that time of the month'

I crash, I deafen my ears

'don't you want babies'

Rain falls from my eyes to my womb

'borderline abnormalities'

My womb a parasite, feeds off my insides

'having an IUD fitted can be uncomfortable'

Silk spun, sharper than daggers

'Blessed is the fruit of thy womb'

I am the mother of living.

A daughter's guide to poaching an egg

Make the water rearrange its insides,

shift shape as it is told,

steam rise

drip drip vinegar,

sour the water to not let things stick.

Watch it fight its way to the surface.

It is not an easy process, such transformation,

if not careful it can erupt, break onto skin that has already learned

this is too hot,

but does it again anyway.

Turn the heat down.

Don't hold the egg too high or it will spread itself open,

reveal itself, some things should be left to the imagination.

Wand a whirlpool and crack it in

watch it bring itself together,

composed, despite itself.

Let the bubbles teach it how to mature,

push it to the surface,

fully fledged

yolk whole, unbroken,

ready for charred bread.

In one move, let the knife cut it open

watch it pour itself out,

ready for hungry tongues.

Solo female traveller

The curve of the blue doorway is
a wide-open mouth, an invitation,
my reflection in the window becomes part of the
shadows that highlight the story of a life,
blades of light frame a bike,
its basket asking to be filled.

One day, I will call a place home,
hold a key that I have two copies of.
Lock the door behind me, turn the heating on,
leave my shoes beside the door,
as dust glitter falls like getting undressed after a night out,
dappled sunlight pushes itself through crimson curtains
demands them to be opened.
I will inhale home, imbibe
let it enter my sinuses,
syllables home heavy,
central heating warm,
I will not fear a rainy day.
My feet warmed in worn, extra-thick,
one striped one not socks stay,
water plants, let the light in,
drink the ancient energy,

let roots grow so long,

so deep they need a bigger pot.

We share oxygen as I dream that

I am a girl with her Canon DSLR,

trying to find the right light for her shot

on emptied old town streets,

before moving on to get the bus to the next city.

Social Mobility

Words fly out of my mouth like little Dianne Abbots, each one a photo
from a Telegraph article about her hairstyles over the years, 'wearing an
afro, making an appointment at the hairdressers.'

The caption reads, so loud I can only say it on repeat.

My words sound like torrential rain on the motorway which means that
I need to leave an extra 3 seconds between me and the person in front of
me.

I think.

Like Dianne I am not good with numbers, but my mistake feels more
dangerous than hers.

I speak my words smaller like 2pt or 3pt, trying to stop them from de-
faulting to Comic Sans but my attempts just turn it into Wingdings which
I think is worse but could also be perceived as artistic which seems like
a good idea sometimes. I change it to Times New Roman, add italics for
emphasis but every time I finish it reverts back.

I wash my mouth out with soap and water like my mom always threat-
ened but never did,

we would always get to the sink and she would make me rinse my mouth
out with my 12 times tables instead which is arguably worse.

The soap I use is 100% from Lush which means I am allowed to use it
and I cannot be responsible for charred orangutans for once and at least
now my words smell nice and not Skol Super instead a mixture of orange
blossom, lavender and cacao.

I add this to my morning routine, in between interdental brushing

and scrubbing my skin clean.

Adult braces

Move the bones in your face, good girl pull

push, conform. Contort, fit the space,

thought there was nowhere to go,

It hurts, so it's working.

Worth it in the end,

deform and fit

into   holes,

swipe right,

smile.

The Universe should come with a fucking instruction manual

He thrusts, frantic like digging dirt
with his hands for treasure, without a map.

Like he does not know our bodies
were there right from the beginning,
more ancient than rocks that worship the sun.

He does not remember
any element in our bodies heavier
than iron, has travelled through
at least one supernova, that a
supernova seeds the next generation of stars,
that stars are all made from the same stuff
so are we.

Are we not supernovas?
I'm trying to show him we are,
we could be
that 4.5 billion years isn't that far, really.

We are as holy as the tide pulled by a womb,
sometimes she burns a blood red orb

so we do not forget, that we were born

to merge as the sea and the shoreline do.

We are as impossible as the light

reflected on faces

emitted from places that

ceased to exist

millions of years ago

yet still they persist.

Still we persist.

But he does not realise that constellations

are stories we tell when the nights

are too dark and we need to

know we are not alone,

we are not the first to do this.

Connected

like protons to neutrons

like yesterday to tomorrow

neuron to neuron to neuron,

our own constellations.

Instead here now, we are together
but as alone as on a road
where streetlights convince us
we are not a part of the universe,
digging with hands,
devouring dirt.

Neural Pathways

The sunrise changes time every day.
    The earth rotates around the sun.
        The stars still burn during daytime.
            This is the meaning of forever.

The sunrise changes time every day.
    The earth rotates around the sun.
        The stars still burn during daytime.
            This is the meaning of forever.
The sunrise changes time every day.
    The earth rotates around the sun.
        The stars still burn during daytime.
            This is the meaning of forever.

The sunrise changes time every day.
    The earth rotates around the sun.
        The stars still burn during daytime.
            This is the meaning of   forever.

The   sunrise   changes   time   every
day.

The earth

rotates

the

sun

Stars   still   burn
during

daytime.

This   is

the

meaning   of   forever.

The   sunrise

changes

the

earth

stars   burn

daytime.

This   is

forever.

Changes

burn

forever.

                                                                          Time

            changes

forever

My sister was born a sunset

When children come out healthy, they are pink.
Or the bit when pink meets red
like that point in the sky
when the sun reminds
of its power to make us forget
everything that came
before it. Even if only a minute.
This blood-spilled sky an ending.
Children are not yellow like a fully-baked sun.

They said she must have jaundice.

My mother tells them her father's
skin holds the burnt ochres of a Caribbean sunset.

They do not say sorry when they hand her over.

Cute

1. Attractive in a pretty or endearing way

The words drop from his lips
stick to my body like flies
open my eyes a tenth of a millimeter wider
raise my voice a tenth of an octave higher.
I know. I reply without actually saying it
because that isn't how it works, that isn't
how this is supposed to work. I paint my
best smile, not too much teeth, I stick out
my bum, suck in my stomach, pull
down my top, arch my back like
the way they taught me.
Look up like when I was a child
watching a cartoon.
Say it again please.

2. Sexually attractive; good looking

He said *when I went out in that top*
it made him upset, his love requires a key,
he wants to give it me but I
am always making it difficult so I

stare through his keyhole mouth when

he says *my stomach would*

be tasty like caramel if only it

would shrink itself.

I wrap myself up in clingfilm

make a hole so I can breathe.

I know how this dance works

with my eyes looking forwards

fixed on one empty lipstick-stained glass

on the table. If I stop moving

can I dance on my own?

3. Clever or cunning, especially in a self-seeking or superficial way.

Like leaving your wallet on the bar

to have it returned empty with no money

you are just glad you got your ID back

it was your fault for getting so drunk and

leaving it there and what were you thinking

buying a wallet so shiny with its mirror

shine silver, paisley pattern

you know that means they would

want to see inside who wouldn't?

So when you run home crying

that they exposed you like you asked and

they laughed at how your body is not

so shiny close up, more silt

what did you expect?

You lazy, lazy thing, next time prepare,

make yourself more girl,

let them take a picture.

You are old

I cradle the blue egg, abandoned like a promise
swathe it in white cotton sheets, let it sleep
warm nest, the airing cupboard.

Watch and wait and watch and wait
and wait and wait

                    and wait.

When she pops through, bald wing first
I do not want to burn her with my fingertips.
she is translucent like milky glass
her veins like mold moving through her hairless body.

I put her in a cage with others her age
so she can speak in bird, which is always
about her dad and when she fell off
the swing and hit her head as a child.
At least I won't feel bad for going to work. I
feed her through a bottle and wonder
was it the egg first or me?

Until one day her wings are

no longer the right shape

bird body bent up against the bars

too big feathers spilling out like a gift

I will lock away in the box I keep her gold earrings,

her bird song a strangled recorder whistle.

And so it is time to let go

I'd like to say I'll see her again

that she will find her way back home

sure as a sea turtle.

But she taught me better than that.

Move on

Ghosts don't exist
except in the lump in the throat
the place between the end
and a new beginning.

What's in an ending?

Endings should justify the beginning
some grand event
encore, chants, applause, eyes salt-stung
more more more

like a hand held as the train pulls away
endings should justify the beginning
or a left behind t-shirt the colour
of the lake we swam in. I hate swimming.

Does the thunderstorm have an ending?
A crescendo? Some grand event
the final crash, a tree burning effigy
or soggied socks?

Does birth end with the
scream of a child, the slime of placenta
encore, chants, applause salt-stung eyes
or is the last push a beginning?

Is it better not to

turn back as the city becomes smoke?

Lot's wife's salt remains a reminder

there are no more more more

goodbyes.

I wanted to keep the plants

I wept for her she was ours but you were not in so my tears fell on cracked soil you were always supposed to be in you promised but you told me promises are only as true as the lips they came from and if the lips are no longer on my pillow were they ever really there? I thank you for teaching me the nature of things that a smell can become cotton fields and tropical rainstorms that futures are real in the moment but live in the past more than anything that futures can be spoke into concrete pillars until the earth opens her mouth to a splinter speaks so only dogs can hear buries them into shadow the earth always knows best I tried to plant our future in barren soil a prayer plant leaves open to collect the sun when the nights grew longer you gave her away to your sister along with my spider plant, aloe, love plant a sick joke, I left the snake plant behind broken she deserved better soil strewn in the road instead of the car I loved her but you did not see a future in our garden no more joined up   dots.

Cleansing ritual

Take the pink plastic razor from Poundland, scrape
you know how they like it Barbie smooth.
Reach right under, don't forget the back
you never know which angle he will see you from.

Whilst you're at it, best do your whole body,
until you are like chicken skin, plucked,
baste yourself in shimmer
ready to sizzle.

He won't notice how you catch under the razor
slicing yourself thinner every time.

Wear a skirt that sucks you in
like you are hourglass sand
each fallen grain a cracked egg.
Spray, walk under a mist of roses and citrus fruit,
practice your walk so he can see you are
girl yet mature
but not too mature.

Forehead shiny like school days
they say you don't look your age
like it's a compliment.

Lay yourself down for him
let him squeeze, he is juicing you.
wear the red marks like a prize.

He has not learned that to extract juice
you must tease it out.
He only knows how to bruise,
he picks apples with his teeth.

Let him, try to take him all in,
drink from each other,
taste, stale roll-up smoke and warm beer
hold it until it erases your words.

Push his arm away and wait for the
sun to shine light on the
dirtied curtains, let it dress your excuses.
Open them,
warm his breath on your skin,
no need for a shower.

Coconut water

They say the coconut kills 150 a year **perhaps I am coconut,**

10 times more likely to kill you than sharks **buoyant adventurer**

rough on the outside, **overwater migrater**

where my dad comes from the coconuts are green, **no-one knows**

they open it with machete add rum **where I came from**

drink down foreign **if you cut me I bleed**

breath like the Portugese language, **coconut-watered plasma**

claims this fruit with its welcoming face **not to everyone's taste**

coconut oil is clean and nourishes; **bounty is always left at the bottom**

elbows dried by harsh winters; **not enough chocolate**

my dad would drag the thin toothed comb **my mother would decorate**

through the knots in my hair, **plaits with beads**

shined with green Dax, **she couldn't do cane-rows,**

he did not know how hair breaks **she said my brothers and sisters were in Africa**

did what he was taught **I thought she had an affair. I wanted to know**

his labour, roots and culture, **were my brothers and sisters like off the T.V**

I'll give you something to cry for, **in between Coronation Street.**

Take of mi belt and beat you, **they would ask me why,**

If you can't hear you must feel, **I drew Katie and not me.**

The last buffet

Cold grey cheese and lukewarm salami
tea followed by strong milky coffee
butter thick-crusted rolls wrapped in tissue,
he would fold so neat, lunch ready for later.

If we had known that would be the last buffet
would we have tried something different?
Instead of the same cold grey cheese and
lukewarm salami every day?

Would we have honey buttered?
Toasted our bread, paused at the
crunch under our teeth floss
the crumbs out of each other with
still hungry tongues, eat jam
with tablespoons, sticky-lipped
and sit still, until we were strawberry-veined
carried each other eight floors
until we fell all limbs into
hotel room, breakfast drunk
then out, try somewhere new
for lunch.

Or would we just have eaten the same

cold grey cheese and lukewarm salami

As we did every day?

As we did every day.

Not everything has to be negative

She, rude as a car's horn at 5.30, dawn
the Northern in her, me
'howay man get the phone'
those work-tired hands
green ink that was once black
tattooed knuckles, Mam
the smell of knock-off cigarettes
they said, *'your house smells like weed'*
I said, *'I know,'* the smell of home
the way her legs dangle
over chair edges like a doll
Rosie and Jim
flip-flopped feet, always too hot
open the windows
Close the windows it's cold mom!
Whiskeyed vowels and consonants
fall over themselves,
I think of the old days
I would listen in front of the door
like an intruder.

I wish I could say the right words
instead of looking at my phone

I don't know why you are never happy.

We watch a documentary about people getting eaten alive by bears, together.

Every child matters

Her voice enters the

room before her

a shark's fist,

always the first

thing before they flood in,

battle-lines drawn

How was your weekend?

I smile, lower a bridge

over the moat she

carries around her, armed with

eye rolls and

why you always picking on me for?

Edge open my drawbridge smile,

each tooth a pearly white flag,

Positive

behaviour

strategy.

We had to run away miss.

Do not let flags drop,

Oh, why was that?

Her voice fills all the

empty space in the room

shadows cover the displays on

4-mark question exam technique,

Explain two contrasting religious beliefs on

the supremacy of God's will.

Her response does not follow

Point Example Explain

she sings her story in verse,

her hymn sheet, the Evening Mail,

she the lead vocalist, 5 others on harmony,

bittersweet chorus,

That's why she isn't in today miss.

The flags fall, the bridge edges back up

Explain two contrasting religious beliefs

on the supremacy of God's will

she rips the pages of her book,

impales them at the top

of broken crockery and rusted knives

That funeral is not an authorised absence

walks her own bridge

her shark's fist,

When am I going to use R.E anyway?

The light goes from the room

I check my emails,

Thanks for reporting.

10 mins later,

That was an inappropriate conversation.

Students should be learning at all times in your classroom.

Just another Friday night

In Grand Central Station, Birmingham
I sat down and waited,
listened to piano chords, a tune
I'm sure I've heard before, a flock of lads
mating call arms spread, ready
'ave it'

The train to Lichfield Trent Valley is delayed by approximately 10 minutes.

I am 20 minutes early.

A man with cigarette burns in brown trousers approaches
holds out stained hands, demands an offering
I hand over a sticky pound from the bottom of my bag
catch myself flinch as I do my best not to touch his
wonder when my skin became so precious.

A gaggle approach, whose skin has not worn
world-weary, walk, wide like they know it too
smooth with the arrogance of youth
I only hope stay that way as long as they can.

A couple walk past, red-haired man shadows over her
throws a ticket on the floor, walks off
a man chases after them, picks it up.

I look at the time, wonder when will the train come.

Gaudi would not have approved

To each strand she whispers, stretch yourself, like straw uncurve. Undo, blend into the empty space they saved you. They told her that it was hers if only she could unbend, make a line of it. They only make space for straight lines: their shelves too full for curl creme '*you are too parched and there is not enough for you to drink, you want to keep drinking*'. There isn't enough space for everyone and her curls take up double. So they pull and they push and use their fingers to touch, make her disappear between the lines, '*We don't have combs with smiles wide open enough to convince your curls into staying*'.   *Sorry.*

Each strand brushed becomes brittle, broken into shards, she sheds, exposed. '*Isn't that better*'? Then she remembers Gaudi. Curves undulating, pieces of broken rainbow toast the naked Catalonian sun. Surrounded by buildings standing straight, in line, trying to bend themselves away from the earth, against their better judgement, doing what they are told over and over again. Until they do not remember they are held together with cement. The Casa Bastillo turns the horizon part kaleidoscope, bent balconies, unfurl against transparent sky to remind her that she is the crest of the ocean, just before it breaks, the deepening curve of a tree's roots, nature's anchor, a freshly-fallen leaf, the fullness of pregnancy, the moon eclipsing the sun and so she tells them of Gaudi. That there are no straight lines   in   nature.

Author Biography

Louise McStravick is a writer, teacher, and proud Brummie. She is a slam winning poet and performer who has headlined at events in London, Birmingham, and Amsterdam including London Literature Festival with Heaux Noire, Beans Rhymes & Life, Streetfest and Words at the Warehouse. She was also part of the very first Apples and Snakes Platform Poets writer development programme, 2020.

She was commissioned to write poems for the Words on Windrush anthology in 2019 with Empoword Slough. This project involved writing poetry based on oral history interviews. As a part of this she was asked read her poetry on BBC Berkshire.

Louise has been published in various places on and offline including, Dear Damsels, Porridge magazine, Tommyrot Zine, Lacuna Lit, Murmaration anthology and an exciting project with Trope publishing that incorporates poetry and photography from London, due to be released in Autumn 2020.

She uses writing to explore the nuances of her mixed-heritage, working-class identity.

About Fly on the Wall Press

A publisher with a conscience.
Publishing high quality anthologies on pressing issues,
chapbooks and poetry products, from exceptional poets around the
globe.
Founded in 2018 by founding editor, Isabelle Kenyon.

Other publications:

(May 2020. Full collection.)
No Home In This World by Kevin Crowe
(June 2020. Short Stories.)

Social Media:
@fly_press (Twitter)
@flyonthewall_poetry (Instagram)
@flyonthewallpoetry (Facebook)
www.flyonthewallpoetry.co.uk

More from Fly on the Wall Press...

Alcoholic Betty by Elisabeth Horan

ISBN10 1913211037
ISBN13 9781913211035

The brave and vulnerable poetry collection of Elisabeth Horan's past relationship with alcohol. Unflinchingly honest, Horan holds a light for those who feel they will not reach the other side of addiction.

"This is the hole. I go there
On Sundays. I go there after dinners
Before school --- mid work day
After lunch with the boss Mondays

The hole has Hangover coal
To paint my face to smudge
In the acne, rosacea, colloscum"

"Alcoholic Betty, we know the story. She died. Or did she? Through the "hours of penance" that is alcoholism and its attendant chaos-math and aftermaths, recurrent false dawns and falsetto damnations, Elisabeth Horan forges a descent/ascension pendulum of fire poems that are not "a map to martyrdom" - but a call to "go nuclear - Repose. Repose." Alcoholic Betty, we know the story. She died. She died so she could live."

- Miggy Angel, Poet, Author and Performer